THE WARRIOR KING

DAVID-LIKE LEADERSHIP FOR GOLIATH-LIKE TIMES

DR. JEFFREY L. SEIF

The Warrior King:
David-like Leadership for
Goliath-like Times

All rights reserved.
Copyright © 2009 by Zola Levitt Ministries, Inc.
P.O. Box 12268
Dallas, Texas 75225-0268
214-696-8844
www.levitt.com

ISBN 978-1-930749-04-7

Table of Contents

Introduction

This book is the work product of an eight-part television series of the same name. Though our ministry's principal niche is the development of on-location television programming in the Middle East, we offer this series transcript as an add-on—a tool to be used independent of the program, or in conjunction with it.

By means of the television medium, this ministry explores the Bible story's various Jewish nuances. We take viewers to and through the Bible lands, and enable them to see the Old and New Testaments with new eyes—as the Jewish people's family diaries. The Old Testament looks forward and the New Testament looks backward. Because both are Jewish in nature, we look at both with decidedly Jewish eyes and offer the resulting perspectives, exploring Jesus' Jewish roots and the prophecies that relate to His first and second comings.

Though *The Warrior King* employs the aforementioned distinctions, it distinguishes itself, in my estimation, for its devotional content.

In this case, it's not just about biblical history or Jesus' story—what is called His-story: it's about you and me. The series is about an emergent faith that arises, gets the better of the days' troubles, and enables those who walk by it to walk victoriously by means of it. Now you have this story in writing.

The transcript has been slightly edited for your easy consumption. I sincerely hope you'll derive a benefit from it, as I did in producing it. I believe that we need David-like leadership for these Goliath-like times. Thanks for traveling with me as I tell you why this is the case and how you can get some of that victorious biblically inspired faith.

Jeffrey Seif   Dallas, TX

1

David's "Call"— and Ours

David's Triumphant Return

Electricity was in the air, if you will. People bristled with excitement: They sensed a new day dawning in Israel. A new personality was emerging. David was beginning to make his mark on Israelite history, and people sensed they'd be the better for it.

It had been hundreds of years since Israel had someone like him. *Moshe Rabbeinu* / Moses, was a religious sort, but he was a spirited soldier. Joshua fired up the national spirit with enthusiasm as he, with his intrepid bold spirit, followed in Moses' footsteps. But after that, the whole thing fell apart. For hundreds of years there wasn't a national hero. People just went to their own homes. They

The Warrior King

went their own way. Israelite life slipped into decay, despair, and disorientation.

Saul held the banner for a season, and it was his job to take the sword out of the sheath and fight Israel's battles. But Saul was independent-minded, and he lost the job. God said, "Enough, already!" Saul proved himself unmanageable, unteachable. He was more concerned about what people thought than about what God thought. God couldn't work with him. And so attention shifted to the House of Jesse where the Lord alighted upon a fellow named David. The word "David" comes from the word meaning "beloved." And beloved David worked his way into the hearts of Israel, and Israel was the better for it. But there was one heart that was not the least bit kindly disposed toward his arrival.

We read in 1 Samuel chapter 18, that following a skirmish with the *Pilishtim* / the Philistines, (we're told in verse seven) that the women came out celebrating with tambourines in hand. And they sang:

הכה שאול באלפו

hika Shaul ba'alafav
"Saul has slain his thousands."

You go, Saul! And then,

ודוד ברבבתיו

V'David beriv'votav
"and David his ten thousands."

Listen to me, Saul was fit to be tied.

David's "Call"—and Ours

I don't know if women understand how much of an effect they have on the male species in so many ways. Saul was so sensitive to how the women perceived him! Being wrapped up in himself as he was, he knew that he was on the outs with God. And when he saw David rise, he became David's enemy henceforth and forevermore, all the way to the grave. Difficulties notwithstanding, against the backdrop of a monarch who was forever trying to kill him, David still rose, growing higher and higher.

My word to you is that you may well have a "Saul" in your life or a set of adversarial circumstances holding you back. Every time you turn around, someone, for reasons of their own, is looking to knock the legs out from underneath you. As we look at *The Warrior King*, we're going to see a story of a man who was not to be stopped. We're going to see a story of a man who overcame adversity, who overcame the "Sauls" in his life. And he had more than one problem. Saul was a perennial one, but when Saul dissipated, there were others.

Difficulties notwithstanding, by the end of David's administration, Israel, which had been 6,000 sq. miles, was then 60,000 sq. miles. How's that for square miles? How's that for growth? Israel was united under one flag and had a strong robust economy. People were prosperous. Israel was a culture of God-seekers. Even David left his mark through song, and many of them were sung in his wake. Under David's administration, people learned that with God they could overcome life's obstacles. In this series, *The Warrior King*, we're going to look at David-like leadership for Goliath-like times, and consider how David's example can inspire us all to walk by faith and get the better of life's vexing dilemmas—something Jesus helps us to do.

The Warrior King

Samuel Anoints David

I believe the New Testament is a very, very Jewish story.
Well, I'm kind of different. Not everybody sees it that way.
The Gospel of Matthew actually was written in Hebrew
first. We only have Greek Text now. It starts off

זה ספר תולדת המשיח ישוע בן־דוד בן־אברהם

zeh sefer toldot Yeshua haMashiach ben David ben Avraham
"this is the book of the genealogy of Jesus Christ, the Son
of David/*ben David*, and the son of Abraham."

I think it's a great story. Jesus Christ… you know when I
grew up I thought his father and mother were Mr. and Mrs.
Christ. Actually Christ itself is a Greek telling of the Hebrew
Mashiach / Messiah. And the word Messiah itself comes
from a word in Hebrew "Anointed One." And why is that?
Because in the Torah there were individuals that when they
came to office they were anointed prophets, priests, and
kings. And they were anointed with oil. And here we are in
an oil-making factory, just like it was in Bible days. And
here the olives are put in and they're ground down. There

are a number of grinding down processes to get the fruit of the olive—that special oil. This is just one contraption here. There are others with pulleys and weights. The name of the game is to harvest that oil, to put the olives under pressure. And you know, on one level it kind of works, to my way of thinking, that leaders get under the olive oil, that which is produced through all this pressure. Because the truth of the matter is, when individuals step up to lead, they step up into a world where there are a lot of pressures.

Our story takes place today against the backdrop of David being visited by *Shmuel*. Samuel the prophet came to *Bet Lechem* / Bethlehem, and he came to the house of Jesse, and he said, "Let me see your boys." "Something tells me I'm in for something good," says Jesse, and those boys are marched one after the other. "I'm planning on anointing one," says the prophet. But, nothing.

Finally, after coming up empty, the prophet looks at Dad and says, "Don't you have anybody else?" "Well, come to think of it we do. We have Davey, that kid out there." To me, it's striking that his own father didn't think highly of him, that David was a loser in his father's eyes, so much so that when the prophet came to the house and said, "Let me see your boys," David wasn't included in the list. And the fact that David is disrespected not just by the father, but by his brothers later on when David comes to the army bringing food staples—talking about taking on Goliath, his brothers say, "Oh shut up David. Who do you think you are? Go tend to your lousy little sheep." The kind of disrespect that David had is striking. God takes this guy out of nowhere—who's a nobody—and brings him somewhere and turns him into a somebody. And let me tell you, that's all about the call of God.

The Warrior King

The rabbis explain why it is that David was so marginalized in his family system. There are various arguments put forth, one of which is that David himself was born out of an adulterous relationship, which would explain why his brothers, who construed their coming into the family more legitimately, would look at him disparagingly. You might recall the Psalm where David said, "In sin did my mother conceive me." And again some rabbis attribute it to just that. Others argue that much as David's grandmother was a Moabitess, so was his mother of non-Jewish extract herself. This could explain why some of the other brothers marginalized David. The reason why some put that forth is because when David was on the run from Saul, he goes and leaves his mom with the Moabites. And that gives credence to that notion.

In any case, we're here in the Text where the prophet comes to the house.

ויאמר יהוה

Va yomer Adonai
"and the Lord said"

קום

Kum
"arise,"

משחהו כי־זה הוא

meshakhehu ki'ze hu
"and anoint him for this is he" (1 Sam.16:12-13).

David, that nobody guy, gets the oil. We're told,

David's "Call"—and Ours

ויקח שמואל את־קרן השמן

vayikakh Shmuel et keren hashemen
"then Samuel took the horn of oil,"

וימשח אתו בקרב אחיו

vayimshakh oto bekerev ekhav
"and he anointed him in the midst of his brethren."

And then,

ותצלח רוח־יהוה אל־דוד

vatitslakh ruakh Adonai el David
"and the Spirit of the Lord fell mightily upon David."

God calls all kinds of people. We have people who are
appointed as leaders, and here we have people who are
anointed. I say three cheers for the call of God. It's
available not just for David and for me, but for you.

The Warrior King

David and Goliath

I remember when I was "called." Speaking of "called," the name I am called by (*"Seif"*) comes from German, meaning "soap." It doesn't bring out a machismo spirit in me to be sure, but my parents are of German-Jewish extract. The word *Seif* has another name in Arabic. It means "sword." I prefer that, but I can't claim that. However, when I think of the faith that I have in the Messiah and in Scripture, I can claim that sword-kind of valiant spirit. The reason is because I want to walk in the footsteps of David.

We are considering a man who, against all odds, jumped into the fray and accomplished great things in life. I believe, by the way, that he needn't be an anomaly. I think all of us can do much the same. David didn't have much to begin with. He didn't have a sword in hand. In fact, David is known for a stone. David didn't kill Goliath with a stone, as is often supposed. He stunned him with it. In fact, I think that Goliath was caught off-guard in so many ways that day. He stunned him with it—knocked him out. And it may well be that as Goliath was coming to, he just lived to see the inglorious moment when he was slain by his own sword. David then took the sword as well as the head as trophies, as booty, as plunder of war. There's a great story there, not that I glory in any death. But I am reminded of the basic biblical principal—this is Bible 101—and that is that faith can, does, and will move mountains. It's all about us at one level. And by that I mean, do we want to exercise faith and get on with the pursuit of the future? The word confidence comes from the Latin word *confides,* a conflation of words meaning "with faith." And I believe, with the Bible characters long ago, that faith works. I really, surely do.

We're looking at a story here where David learned it (that basic biblical principle) that day on the field of battle. And let me tell you that so many things in life are really learned on the field of battle. If we want to have a testimony for the Lord, well that's great. It's good to have a testimony. But if we're going to have a *testimony*, we have to have a *test* first. Life presents us with a lot of challenges, but challenges are opportunities in work clothes. We just have to rise up and meet them head on. And David did that, didn't he? Others were afraid. They were daunted by this towering Goliath. But David really thought that the bigger they were, the harder they fall. And he just jumped into the fray and the rest is history.

In the book *Shmuel*, in Samuel chapter 17—I want you to read with me here—we're told

ויאמר דוד אל־הפלשתי

Va yomer David el ha Pilishti
"then David said to the Philistine…"

—and, by the way, no reference here to individuals who today refer to themselves as Palestinians, individuals of Arabic extract. The reason why I say that is the *Pilishtim* themselves were a seafaring people who came in from the Greek mainland or the Greek islands and they moved this way and they were held at bay. Arab cousins to the Jewish people who've come up from Saudi Arabia from the east and moved in—these aren't the original Palestinians to speak of, though the name endures today. So this isn't a story here about Jews against the Arabs; no, this is David against the real genetic Philistines. In any case, then said David to the Philistines

אתה בא אלי בחרב

Atah bah ehli b'kherev

"you come to me with sword and spear and javelin," etc.

But then, what he says as a follow up is just emblazoned in biblical memory:

ואנכי בא־אליך בשם יהוה צבאות

v'ahnochi bah ehlecha b'shem Adonai tsehva'ot

"but I come to you in the name of the Lord of hosts,"

יהוה צבאות

Adonai tsehvaot

"the Lord of the armies" (1 Samuel17:45).

I want you to hear me for a second. We live in precarious times. And I'm not just speaking about world culture and individual nation-states. The world is a very precarious place, and various nations are in the throes of despair in so many ways. When I think of household units that are basic building blocks of any society, just like this pillar here is holding up this house, so too the family is a basic building block. The family is being assailed. There are challenges today. Well, who is or isn't president isn't as important. What social programs are on the table, isn't as important. What's important is that we, like David, rise up with faith. Because I believe that faith can and will pay dividends: faith in Jesus, Israel's Messiah.

The Warrior King

2

David and Saul
And the challenges for us all

Saul Tries to Kill David with a Spear

I am sure that it was extremely painful for David, and I want you to get the point as well because it can be extremely painful for us. What's that, pray tell? When we are not only abandoned by friends and associates, not only disappointed, but outright betrayed, it's tragic. Sometimes there are people whom we serve well, and in response we are not just disrespected, but they unleash forces upon us that would knock the legs out from underneath us. Sometimes we can take our friends and weigh them in the scales, and they can come up wanting. Why is that? Because, much as we try to love them, they come after us with a vengeance. And that's tragic, isn't it, that we have to be on the defensive, that we have to be on the ready against friends, people whom we serve and love? That's where the Warrior King David— well, he's not a king yet—but that's where he finds himself.

And maybe this is his training on the way to being the king. What do I mean by that? You know the story. David entered into a world against the backdrop of Saul's demise. Saul was vested with authorization to be the king, to lead the people, but he wasn't leading the people. He was bleeding the people. He was feeding off of them instead of feeding them. Why is that? Well, it was all about the House of Saul. It was all about him benefiting from the position that he had instead of using his energies to benefit the community. Well, God finally says, "I can't work with this man anymore. He just won't repent. He's not teachable." So the words to Saul from the prophet *Shmuel*, is "Enough already!" The Lord turned to someone else—David. And He found in him stock that He could raise up and could use.

Now what's interesting—part of David's being raised up was his having this titanic struggle with the man whom he began serving. And isn't that tragic? I don't know if you've ever found yourself in a place where the world has turned on you. Here we're in a home where there's some love. People are working together. You've heard the expression that a man's home is his castle. The reason for that is that sometimes the world outside can be so very precarious, very tumultuous. We retreat into the confines of our own home. But what do you do when your own home, your own safety zone, turns on you? David had that happen to him. His whole world turned upside down. He learned to rely on God. But the same God he was relying upon was the one who was counted upon to send him troubles. Why do I say

David and Saul

that? If you look in 1 *Shmuel* chapter 19, we're told in verse 9,

ותהי רוח יהוה רעה אל־שאול

Vatehi ruakh Adonai ra'a el Shaul
"and an evil spirit from the Lord came upon Saul."

I don't know that God's in the business of dispatching demons. The point is, the Lord allowed it to happen. Why is it that the Lord allows bad things to happen to good people, or why does He allow His people to have bad people assault them? Well, we learn to trust in Him, to be sure. It seems to me that if we're going to be champions, we have to learn to bear underneath difficult burdens and weights, and that makes us in the process.

David was a king. He had to learn his craft and learn about trusting in God and about how He can deliver from bad people and bad circumstances. David learned that, and he became the warrior. He was forged in the furnace of affliction. There were many things that David learned, by the way, because of the difficulties that he experienced, difficulties that served him well. And I want you to know that the difficulties you experience in life, if you're walking with the Lord, can serve you well as well. Scripture says that "all things (even "Saul" things) work for the good of those who love God and who are called according to His purpose" (Romans 8:28).

I have a Saul in my life—one or two, to tell you the truth, and you probably do as well. But you know what? If you have the Lord in your life, that's plenty good to get the better of life's challenges. It's sometimes easy to feel alone, isn't it, when you feel you're running away from people's fears?

The Warrior King

But that's not all the story with Saul and his family. If you read the Bible, you learn that Saul had a son *Yonatan /* Jonathan, a man of a different sort altogether. It's interesting; inasmuch as Saul was hell-bent on destroying David, David had endeared himself to Jonathan, not only as a best friend, but as a great friend. We're going to look at him in a moment. But even Saul's daughter fell in love with David. Go figure! An upside-down world, isn't it? Sometimes an upside-down world is the kind of world that God uses to get His people right side up.

And so, when we look at the story of our Warrior King David, we learn about Davidic leadership in Goliath-like times, and we learn how He used difficulties to make that man who he was. In conjunction with those difficulties, blessings were to be found.

David and Saul

David and Jonathan

The word fraternity comes from the Latin word *frater*, which means "brothers." As you may recall from the biblical Text — *hinei matov umanaim shevet akhim gam yakhad* / "behold how good and pleasant it is when brethren dwell together in unity"—that people need people (Psalm 133:1). *Yeshua* / Jesus, is on record saying, "By this all men will know that you are My disciples, by your love for one another," by your fraternity (John 13:35).

When I think of the story of *David and Yonatan* / Jonathan and David, I'm reminded of a relationship that is just fantastic. And, by the way, it's rare among men these days—outside of the theater of combat, I should say. Men forge bonds when they go off to war and struggle together against a common foe. I never served in the army, but I have a career in law enforcement, and I know that there's a kind of fraternal bond among men who bear arms in defense of home and hearth in the police force. There's a lifelong bond that cops share. And, by the way, it's so all

17

over the world. I can go to another continent and talk to a cop about cop stuff. We are instant buddies. There's something about braving the same kinds of hazards that forms bonds. And men need those bonds. Males develop relationships in war where they learn to work together, cultivating skills of reliance and responsibility. And then we leave that world and return to civilian life where it's every man for himself. There's something tragic in that! Males feel something missing. There's a vacuum, something that needs fixing. And why is that? Because a man is alone, and men were not made to be alone. As strange as that might sound, there's a void in the heart of a man that can't be filled by a woman. I know I can be misunderstood by saying that (it wouldn't be the first time, and I can get bad mail), but it's true. Men need men. And that can be problematic, because ain't it like the devil to sexualize that. When I look here in the sacred Text to see about the sacred bond between men, let's not even think of sexualizing that! I believe the Bible legitimizes relationships between Adam and Eve, not Adam and Steve.

But I want you to see this. In *Shmuel*, 1 Samuel chapter 20 and verse 16:

ויכרת יהונתן עם־בית דוד

vayikhrot Yonaton im beit David
"and Jonathan made a covenant."

כרת בריתו

Cherot b'ritoh
He "made a covenant" with David.

18

David and Saul

And we're told in verse 17, "*Yonatan* caused David to swear for the love that he had for him, for he loved him as he loved his own soul."

I believe there's a longing for that, by the way. I believe there's a need for that. I can't tell you how, as a police officer, I would love just to sit around in uniform with other men. Maybe there was a fight—an incident, something we worked together to break up—and then there's a kind of camaraderie where we connect and process what happened. Oh for the joy of that! To me, it's tragic how that's missing outside of that culture. You know, I've had some experience serving as a firefighter as well, where we debrief, we don the bunker gear. You know, most people are smart enough to run from a fire; some people are dumb enough to run into it. I say that tongue in cheek, of course—they're not dumb, they're heroes! The point is that when people work together in a common cause and common struggle, it forges alliances that wouldn't otherwise be there. And we need that. I believe that God's people need to recover that.

And there are different fraternal associations. In North America, Promise Keepers is ramping up again. Coach [Bill] McCartney has resumed the helmet along with Raleigh Washington, two men who love Israel, love the Jewish people, and who love Messianic Jews, I might add. Promise Keepers is again going to take the world by storm. And local congregations would do well to provide opportunities for men to link up with men. The Bible says, *hinei matov umanaim shevet akhim gam yakhad* / "how good and pleasant it is when brothers dwell together in unity" (Psalm 133:1).

The Warrior King

Here me, mister! You might have a lot of talent, but you are not going to excel, you're never going to become what you could otherwise be, if you forever want to go it alone in life. Find good friends. Cultivate those bonds. Be faithful to each other. David and Jonathan did that. It's a moving story. Never mind my words, read the Bible itself and learn how David was the better for his association with Jonathan.

It actually seems that David benefited from associations with both the father and the son. Though one gave him grief and the other joy, his respect for both is amply attested in what he said about both in his parting words.

David and Saul

Saul Kills Himself with his Sword

The expression "to fall upon one's sword" speaks of someone taking his own life. We're at a place in David's life where he's learned that his nemesis has fallen upon his own sword. Saul is dead, and Jonathan along with him.

For my money, Saul could have died a lot sooner. That would have been okay, because, the God's honest truth, I didn't like that man as soon as I met him in biblical literature. At least, not long after I read it, I realized there was something wrong with that man. Jonathan, on the other hand—you just can't help but fall in love with. I love that guy, and I say that at the risk of being misunderstood. In any case, David here is confronted with the fact that both are dead. And it's monumental in the biblical Text—the Samuel Text is clear—that David had every reason to want to kill Saul, but he never exercised his prerogative. David's conduct is sterling. And why is that? Because he wouldn't take it upon himself to be given to executing his superior officer in that social system. He spends 13 years *not*

The Warrior King

fighting Saul, but *running from him*. And now, as he's
running, he's overrun with the fact that Saul is dead.

We come upon that story in 1 *Shmuel* / 1 Samuel chapter
31, very simply in verse four, at the end. Saul and the army
are engaged in a clash with the *Pilishtim* / with the
Philistines, and it doesn't go Saul's way. And we're told
finally in verse 4:

ויקח שאול את־החרב ויפל עליה

vayikakh Shaul et hakherev vayipol aleiha
"therefore Saul took his sword and he fell upon it."

He was mortally wounded and he said, "Enough already."
The battle's gone horribly. He experiences the death of his
own around him. And, by the way, that's life's worst insult,
to see your friends and your family die in front of you.

Saul just says, "Enough already." He knew he was a dead
man, actually. Years beforehand, the Lord had approached
him through the prophet saying, "Listen, the kingdom is
being taken from you. Your house is not going to endure."
And he resisted and resisted, and finally God's will overran
him. It's tragic, at one level. We're told then in verse 7,
very simply:

וכי־מתו שאול ובניו

vekhi me'tu Shaul uvanav
"Saul and his sons were dead."

What's interesting, for my money, is the way that David
responded. As I've said, the way I perceive it, Saul could
have died a lot earlier, and that would have been okay. I
imagine David could have been tempted to just breathe a
deep sigh of relief, but it wasn't the nature of the guy.

David and Saul

David—and this is really interesting, I think, and it's evident. You'll hear David in his own words—he was mournful over it. David had been running from that man for 13 years. And you know what? God used that tough guy to grow up David. God used the "Saul"—He used it all: wars with his own, wars with the Philistines—God used it all to make that man the man that he became.

And great leaders are great bleeders. That is to say, we all have scars under our shirts, and they make us the people we are. David's leadership was forged in the furnace of challenge. David makes peace with his nemesis, if you will. You know, there's the old Spanish expression, *Adios*, which doesn't mean "goodbye." It is goodbye, but it means "to God." And I think that David gave his struggles over to God a long time beforehand, and now he eulogies Saul and Jonathan. I want you to hear this, in 2 Samuel chapter one, he says in verse 23, "Saul and Jonathan, the lovely and the pleasant." How can David describe Jonathan and his father as the lovely and the pleasant? You know how? You can be vexed over somebody who's really been messing you up for years, but you make peace with it. And you say, "God, whatever." I think it's striking that David himself did much the same. He says in verse 26, "I'm distressed for thee, my brother Jonathan." David learned to forgive and give it over to God. And he was able to go on to greatness. Would that we did likewise.

The Warrior King

3

David's Family
Affairs and troubles brought to bear

David Runs from Absalom

Jews construe that it's imperative for a father to teach his son a trade and to see that he learns the religion as well. That is, the burden is on the father to inculcate certain things in the next generation. And in this regard, it's sad to say, David failed miserably. And why is that? Because David had too many sons. Twenty sons are noted in First and Second Samuel, and one daughter. Beyond that we're told that he had other wives and other children that aren't even noted by name. The man had too many women.

Moshe Rabbeinu / Moses warned, I believe in *Devarim* / in Deuteronomy, that kings will tend to multiply women to

25

themselves. David had a family that was too big to manage, and he wasn't given to managing his own family. The net result was that he, who could forge a kingdom, failed at home. And isn't that, by the way, a tragic story that is seen played out way too many times today? The men go off and they conquer in various ways, but the children are neglected. I mention this here because it is a tragic fact that David's sons turned on him. I'm a dad, and I've raised sons. The Lord has seen fit to grace me with boys. Oh, for the love of God, it scares me to think how I'd feel if my boys turned on me. For me, I like to be respected, personally. If I feel I'm disrespected at work or wherever, it bothers me. It's my Achilles heel. And if I feel like I'm being disrespected at home, that is particularly offensive. *Rav Shaul* / the Apostle Paul alighted upon that when he said, "Wives, respect your husbands." Then he said, "Husbands, love your wives." The respect factor is significant.

Well, the story in this segment is played out against the backdrop of David not only being disrespected by his sons, but being forced to flee as one of those sons—and it's not just one; in various ways on various days, different ones weighed in—looked to undermine David. Absalom was particularly egregious. It wasn't just that he was bent on revolt, he mobilized others to knock the legs out from under his father, David, and then to usurp his own father's authority and take the kingdom.

We read in First and Second Samuel about David's rise and demise. We discover that he was forced to flee. There's a tragic Text here. I can't read all of it. And by the way, much as I'm pleased that you're giving me a hearing on nationally syndicated television, more important than me is the biblical Text itself. My value is only in my being able to

David's Family

contribute to your understanding of it. My encouragement to you would be to get into the Bible. The Holy Spirit can guide you into all the truth. You don't need me as your schoolteacher, but I thank you for tuning in.

Now, tune into this—a piece of tragedy in the written Word. In 2 Samuel 15:13, we're told:

ויבא המגיד אל־דוד לאמר

vayavo hamagid el David le'mor
"and a messenger came to David saying,"

היה לב־איש ישראל אחרי אבשלום

haya levish Yisrael akharei Avshalom
that "the hearts of the men of Israel are inclined toward Absalom."

Absalom, were he to have had his way, would have been David's undoing. The truth of the matter, and David knew the truth of the matter, and that is that Absalom really wasn't his problem. The problem was that David sinned, and he was now reaping what he had sown. He wasn't faithful within the confines of his own marriage contracts. He let it all get away from him, and now he's reaping the harvest.

There's much in the biblical literature to commend that is positive, but here's a story that is negative. Have you ever heard the expression that a wise man learns from his mistakes? Well, that's true; but a wiser man learns from somebody else's. Better it is that we learn from David and not repeat his mistakes. And why do I say that? David couldn't take care of his sexual business: he had too many women, too many kids, until it all got away from him. He experienced God's grace, to be sure, and was forgiven. But still, the consequence of all that he had done played out. Now listen to me, everyone within the sound of my voice. We all possess a human nature. Better it is, it seems to me, that we get on top of our business so that we don't have to go this way, so that we can have strength in the family. All said, I want you to know that there is a grace available to you. God is so very good! David finished his days well, difficulties notwithstanding, and you can finish well, too. But learn a lesson from David, the Warrior King.

David's Family

Abigail Pleads Before David

I am reminded that, great though David the king was, he was still a man who was subject to human frailty. He was indeed imperfect. His acting in a less than perfect manner is underscored in the book *Shmuel* / Samuel. It's a book that's named after its writer, although he didn't write it all. The reason why [we know this] is because in the 25th chapter, where we are today, he dies. And this man's death precipitates a crisis for David—because it had been *Shmuel* who launched his career—we're told in 1 Samuel chapter 25, verse 1:

וימת שמואל

vayamat Shmuel
"and Samuel died,"

ויקבצו כל־ישראל

vayikavsu kol Yisrael
"and all Israel gathered themselves to him,"

The Warrior King

ויספדו־לו

Vayispe'du lo
"and they lamented him."

We're told that shortly thereafter:

ויקם דוד וירד אל־מדבר פארן

vayakam David vayered el midbar Paran
after that "David leaves and goes to the wilderness of
Paran."

And when he goes there, David is still reeling somewhat
from the news of the death of his mentor. And, as if that
wasn't bad enough for the man, as with this wagon, he was
very low on provisions, in many respects empty, in fact.

So David went, and the story's unpacked in the 25th chapter.
David followed the conventions of the day. He went back
to someone who should have been a patron to him. David
and his men weren't out acting as brigands, stealing off the
land; but rather they were policing. His men were out and
about—granted, on the run from Saul—but they were
protecting various estates in the wilderness and in the
countryside. Decorum had it that those who protected
should be able to go back and get some basic provisions.

Similarly, I have a career as a police officer, and I work as
a cop, usually late at night. It wasn't at all uncommon that
I'd pull into a gas station and they'd give me some coffee.
They were glad that I pulled in there. These stop-and-go
gas stations get robbed all the time, and police presence is
good. So, they're happy to feed me a little bit and give me
some beverage just for me coming in there. Similarly,
David's men were acting, in effect, as police officers.

David's Family

David was running low on provisions, and he went to one fellow named Nabal / *Nabal*, which means "fool,"—and if anyone ever lived up to his name, he did—and David asked him if he could help him out a little bit. It's the equivalent of a tip. Is he required to tip? No. Are you required to tip the waitress or the waiter? No. But you do. What happened is that Nabal didn't. And I imagine that what happened next was because David was feeling a little rudderless. He had just lost his mentor and was feeling like a tailless kite in the sky. He doesn't have stability. When word gets to him that his men and he were disrespected by Nabal, David was fit to be tied. He went into a rage and said, "Every man gird up your sword on your thigh." And David went to kill him.

Think of that for a minute. This fellow, in a flash of rage and consternation, is ready to go shed innocent blood. Now, it may well be that a guy like Nabal isn't fit to live, and you might have some people in your webs of relationships that are like Nabal. You feel so mistreated by them, so misunderstood, so disrespected, you just know that your world would be a better place if they weren't in it. Well, you know what? That may be true at some level, but it's not your job to be judge and jury. There's a greater Judge.

In any case, as an extension of his own rage and angst, David went after him to kill him. Abigail, Nabal's wife, hears of this and goes to bring provision to David, treating him very, very respectfully, with the net result that David's anger is waylaid. This is extremely important. When David realizes that Abigail saved him from shedding innocent blood, he says in 1 Samuel 25:32,

The Warrior King

ויאמר דוד לאביגל

vayomer David la Avigal
"and David said to Abigail,"

ברוך יהוה אלהי ישראל

barukh Adonai Elohei Yisrael
"Blessed be the Lord God of Israel,"

אשר שלחך היום הזה לקראתי

asher shelakhekh hayom haze lik'rati
"who has sent you this day to meet me."

David was smart enough to allow himself to be instructed.
And I want you to hear me on this. As great a man as David
was, he wasn't too great to get some advice from a woman.
Would that we similarly were open to advice from all kinds
of places and allowed ourselves to be led by others. We
would do well to allow ourselves to be led by our
consciences as well, would we not?

David's Family

David and Bathsheba

"David, David, David," I've wondered. How could you? "You're a good enough sort, I'll grant; but in your fifties, sir, you surely lost your way." This was evidenced one evening, was it not? He should have been out with his armies. God anointed him to lead, to invest his energies in solving Israel's problems. But no, apparently he retired prematurely and then experienced some troubles of his own.

It's sad to say. In the previous segment, we looked at how David was bested by anger after his mentor died. He is ready to kill someone just for an insult. And here he's going to kill someone just to mask his own indiscretions. David, David, David. How could you do it? Well, the fact that David could do it, tells me that so could I, and if we're gut-level honest, so could you. David never did anything that I haven't thought of. Now, I'm not trying to do confession on national television. The point is that I'm a man. I'm shackled with a human nature. We have to keep this business under control.

Our story takes place in 2 Samuel chapter 11, one evening when David let the cat out of the bag. In verse 2:

ויהי

vayehi
"And it came to pass,"

לעת הערב

Le'et ha'erev
"in the evening,"

ויקם דוד מעל משכבו

vayakam David me'al mishkavo
"and David arose from his bed."

ויתהלך על־גג בית־המלך

Vayit'alekh al gag beit hamelekh
"and he walked on the roof of the king's house,"

וירא אשה רחצת מעל הגג

vayar isha rokhetset me'al ha gag
"and he saw a woman bathing."

Was David being a little voyeuristic up there? No doubt. Could Bathsheba have been a little more careful down there? No doubt. Somewhere between the two, there was an accident. There was a spark that was ignited. And it set fire to a household that tore up many a room and many people in them. We're told,

David's Family

וְהָאִשָּׁה טוֹבַת מַרְאֶה מְאֹד

veha'isha tovat mar'e me'od

"and the woman he saw was very beautiful to look upon."

David, David, David. He saw, he took. When he found out later that his one-night stand was in danger of being exposed because Bathsheba was pregnant, he then hatches a scheme to try and mask his indiscretion. Uriah was such a good sort of fellow, a loyal soldier. He wouldn't sleep with Bathsheba because his men were in the field at the front. And so, David sent him back to the front carrying orders for his own execution. David told his general, "Take that guy Uriah, put him in the front of the battle, then withdraw the troops and let him fall. And so it was, he did. And the rest is history.

David's then going to marry Bathsheba. Oh, David, David, David. For the love of God, man, how can you do it? This is a dark side in an otherwise illustrious career. And this program alights upon it. That is to say, in the previous segment we saw how David, in a knee-jerk response to an insult, would launch off to kill. And here, in a knee-jerk response to a temptation, David will seize and then kill. We'll look in the third segment at how David reaped a harvest because of his indiscretion, because of his inability to rein it in.

Let me encourage you with something. It could very well be that a program like this, that goes into millions of homes…. I know that there are some of you, when I talk about sexual indiscretion within the home, for some that hits pay dirt. Now listen to me, I don't want to make you feel guilty. What I want you to do is experience the forgiveness that David experienced. Even a good man like

35

The Warrior King

David got himself into a lot of trouble. Here's what you need to do. It says in the Scriptures that "if we confess our sins, He is faithful and just and will forgive us of all unrighteousness" (1 John 1:9). Let me encourage you to do that. Let me encourage you, as well, to not only be honest with God, but be honest with another. Visit your pastor. Get on your knees. Reach up to God. There's a great and glorious future for you. David learned that God's grace even covered this.

4

David's Wars
And the Spirit that helped him get the better of them

David Battles the Philistines

News crews don't come here much anymore. But I have news for you. Years ago this place was the talk of the town. I have to be careful as I drive here now because we're reasonably high up, and I don't want to just look at the camera. I need to look at the road.

Behind me is the Valley of Elah, the place where David sparked a revolution, if you will. For the longest time, Israelites were oppressed; so pressed, repressed, depressed, and impressed with the recognition that something needed to change. And why was that? Because the *Pilishtim* were working havoc over here. And not just the Philistines here, but different "stines" at different places. People were afraid. They were ready for a change. Talk about "we need change." Well, they really wanted it. They needed it, and the time was right. Someone needed to stand up with some faith, some *biblical* faith. A lot of people have a lot of ideas about what needs to happen in the world. But you know what? Finally, someone stood up with God's idea. And I love him for doing that. By virtue of his so doing, David left a mark on biblical literature, not only in his own day, but extending thousands of years later. It all started here. What a fitting place to tell the story of the need to contend and war, if you will, for God's sake. For the most part, the implications for us are spiritual more than material. But we need to recover that radical edge, and I want to talk to you about that edge as we look at *The Warrior King* and we consider the need for David-like leadership in these Goliath-like times.

Speaking of the cutting edge, I'm reminded of a rather interesting verse—a Scripture that might seem somewhat offensive at face value. 1 Samuel chapter 17 verse 54: it says in Hebrew,

ויקח דוד את־ראש הפלשתי

vayikakh David et rosh ha Pilishti
"and David took the head of the Philistine,"

ויבאהו ירושלם

vayeviehu Yerushalayim
"and he took the head to Jerusalem."

It goes on to say that he took Goliath's armor and put it in his own tent. It seems to me that we're looking here at the

David's Wars

Warrior King. He's not a Warrior King at this juncture. He's a young man who opted to jump into the fray, who later became a king because the culture was looking for a man of faith who was going to stand up and lead, and maybe risk a little bit in the process of so doing. Well, David certainly jumped into the fray. I'm sure it was unexpected. But all of a sudden, he found himself where the troubles of the day afforded him the opportunity to rise and be what God had called him to be. I don't know about you, but there's something about this imagery that really works for me.

We live in a unisex world where gender boundaries are blurred. There are a number of things that are blurred in this upside-down world of ours. But I'm looking here at a male who wants to believe God, and stand up and be counted. He wants to be heroic, if you will. I believe that we live in a world where heroism is in very high demand, but very short supply.

When I look at David, I'm not only reminded of an image from his Philistine wars, I'm not only reminded of an image of what he was all about, but I see here an image of what we ought to be all about, as men particularly, and people of faith generally. That is, stand up. Don't just accept the taunts of the enemy. So many people are beaten into submission, and they despair and they pray up. They send their prayers heavenward, and I'm all for that, and I do that on more than one occasion. But what about "stand-up guys"? I believe that we need this David-like leadership today. We need men to stand up and be men as men, men to stand up and be men as husbands, men to stand up and be men as fathers, men to stand up and be men as pillars of their congregations, men to be men and stand up for their city, for their county, for their state, and for their country. I believe that we need biblical leaders who want to make the world better by virtue of their participating in the drama. David, as a leader, invested his energies with the net result that Israel was better because of his plying his skill sets within the culture. And would that today people caught that vision—that they wanted to lead, they wanted to make the world a better place, their family a better place, their congregations a better place, and culture as a whole. We need to pray up and stand up, now more than ever. As we look at the world, let's look at it with biblical eyes and come to terms with the fact that we need David-like leadership for these Goliath-like times.

Dr. Jeffrey Seif at Khirbet Qeiyafa, Israel, near the Valley of Elah.

Oldest Hebrew script ever found, dating to the period of David

David's Wars

David Receives the Ephod

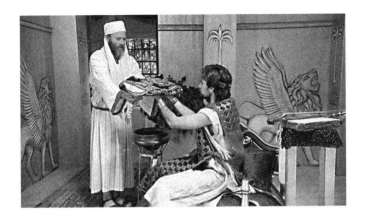

When filming in Israel, we go to places where tour buses can't go and where cars often don't. In fact, my four-by-four, off-road vehicle couldn't even get to one place. And where was that? We filmed in a place that I wasn't planning on taking you to. I wasn't planning on being there myself. I didn't know about this place a week ago. I came here to Israel to shoot a series called *The Warrior King* on David. Little did I know that in conjunction with our arrival and filming we would have one of the greatest modern discoveries in the history of biblical archaeology. I know it sounds overstated, but it isn't: Articles are appearing in major Israeli periodicals, on the Internet. Right here in the northeastern hills of Elah, in the ruins of Qeiyafa, we have a fortress that dates back to 1,000 BC.

Now what makes this find striking—and I'm coming to you from the middle of it—what makes it striking is the fact that right here, very recently, were unearthed the oldest Hebrew scripts found to date, predating the discovery of the

The Warrior King

Dead Sea Scrolls by almost a millennium. And that's striking for a variety of reasons. Why is that? Because this was a fortress that dates back to the era of David. That's significant because we live in a world today when there are many revisionist sorts who are trying to rewrite history. Just as we hear in America, "Oh, it wasn't really a Christian country originally," some want to rewrite history in order to foist their agenda on modernity. Similarly in Israel, there are individuals who are looking for a disconnect from biblical heritage. "Well, there never was a King David," they say. Well, it was harder to say that when, up north some years ago, an inscription to the House of David was found, right there at Tel Dan in the far north. And now, here in a fortress that dates back to David's day, we find Hebrew script. This is interesting in part because the fact that there would be a Hebrew fort here—it's an extension fort—argues for a strong kingdom in Jerusalem. This was an outpost here that was established not far from where the biblical story played out once upon a time when David went against *Goliat* / Goliath. It's a great story. Biblical history is interesting. And we find that modern archaeology in various ways corroborates the biblical narrative. What's happening here at this site argues to that effect.

But my purpose here isn't to talk about biblical archaeology, fascinating as it is. I want to raise the story of David, in part because we need to hear from him and learn from him today. I'd like you to turn in your Bibles, please, to 1 Samuel. There's an interesting story here when things weren't going David's way. It just so happens in life that sometimes culture turns against us, circumstance turns against us, and we find ourselves being pushed back. David was disconcerted when he discovered that his town was overrun, his family was taken captive—everything was taken in fact. People were

so mad at him as a leader, they were ready to stone him!
We're told in the Hebrew Bible, chapter 30 verse 6,

ותצר לדוד מאד

vatetser le David me'od
"David was greatly distressed"

because of the defeats that he had experienced just then. And
people, we're told, were ready to stone him. Leadership is
very precarious, just like standing here is precarious.
Sometimes the winds blow for you, sometimes against you.
David was on the downside of it all. But we're told here in
the Text,

ויתחזק דוד ביהוה אלהיו

vayitkhazek David ba Adonai Elohav
"David strengthened himself in the Lord his God."

For those of us who want to be good leaders, we have to
fall on our knees sometimes because the truth of the matter
is that there are challenges. And what happened? David
strengthened himself. He called for the priest to bring
garments. He wanted to consult the Lord, actually. And as
we read in verse 8 we're told,

וישאל דוד ביהוה

Va'nish'al David ba Adonai
"and David inquired of the Lord."

He had questions. He didn't know how to respond. And
you know, we live in a world today where we can be beset
by circumstances that don't seem to be going our way. We
need to seek the Lord as well. The good news is that if we
do, if we seek Him, we'll find Him. And we'll find answers
for vexing human dilemmas.

The Warrior King

Syrian Kings Bow Before David

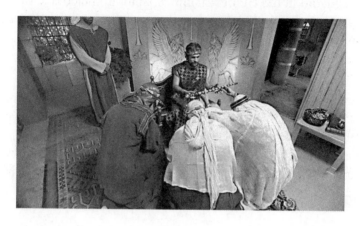

There were lots of helicopters and jets flying around the day I shot this section of the program by the Gaza. I don't have enough clout to make them stop. We're 40 kilometers from the Gaza, and that's probably the reason why they're busy out and about doing what they're doing. Here we are, doing what we're doing: visiting a famous site in antiquity, an outpost for David's forces right at the border with the *Pilishtim* / the Philistines. And it's interesting, by the way, that today there are problems with individuals who use the name "Palestinian."

And so it is that overhead, individuals are maintaining vigilance in the skies, just as—from where I'm standing— years ago, individuals maintained vigilance as well, to fight off the prevailing darkness. And fight we must, by the way. I mean that in the truest of senses. Not all of us bear arms in defense of home and hearth. But anyone who names the Name of the Lord is called to arm-up, if you will, to put on the helmet, the shield, and get out the sword of the Spirit

David's Wars

(Ephesians 6:16, 17). We're vested with the responsibility to contend, to stand for principles. And, in the course of fighting, we should know that it doesn't always go our way. Sometimes, as David learned on more than one occasion, we need to strengthen ourselves in the Lord. And, by the way, I think this is that sort of time.

I'm reminded, when I read 2 Samuel chapter 10, David was involved in a battle royal. The end result was that the individuals came and did subservience to him. He got the better of it. And the kings came and bowed down. Peace at last. But before that, he had to contend, and in chapter 10 verse 12,

חזק ונתחזק
khazak venitkhazak
"be of good courage and let us be strong."

Now friends, that's a word for today. He says,

בעד־עמנו
Be'ad amenu
"be strong for our people,"

ובעד ערי אלהינו
uve'ad arei Eloheinu
"and for the cities of our God."

At 53 years of age now, I realize that I've lived a good part of my life. I'm not ready to stick myself in the grave, but I realize that the better part of it is in the rear-view mirror. I plan to finish well. I feel, in so many ways, I'm not just fighting for myself as much as for my kids, as much as for future generations. I believe that God's people today, we need to be strong. We need to be serious. We need a

45

revival. We need a renewal of energies and enthusiasm to do the Lord's bidding. It feels like the battle isn't going our way. And you know what, in ways it isn't. But I've seen enough football games to realize that the winning team may be at a loss at halftime, but it's not over until the bell rings at the end of the fourth quarter. I don't believe it's over for America, but I do believe that there are a number of challenges now.

That said, when I read the Bible I'm reminded of the fact that these guys always had struggles. That's the bad news. The good news is to hark back to Paul's word, "Thanks be to God who leads us to triumph" (2 Corinthians 2:14). I would like your faith to be built up. I know mine needs building up as well. And here, coming from a fort, an outpost of David's empire 3,000 years ago, I want to encourage you in your faith. I believe that we need David-like leadership in Goliath-like times. Will you stand with me and be that man of God and that woman of God, and help our culture return to its biblical moorings?

5

The Celebrated Warrior King

David is Anointed as King

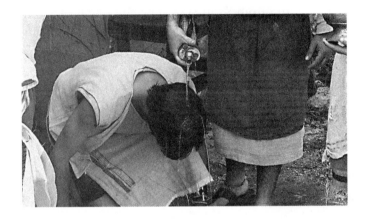

I visited the City of David. At the southern part of what's known as the Temple complex today lie ruins that have been here for centuries. Some decades ago they began to be unearthed. Kathleen Kenyan, a famous archaeologist, put her ax into the soil here, as have others, to try to reconstruct David's palace. And I'm coming to you, yes, from the Acropolis, the very place, if you can imagine that. One of the benefits of teaching here from Israel is that we don't just tell the Bible story, we can give individuals a window into it. And what a story this is.

I wonder what David would have felt like, frankly. He'd been on the run from Saul for the better part of 13 years, if you can imagine that. It had been a long time since *Shmuel* showed up and anointed him, called him out from his father, set him up in the midst of his brothers, and said, "You have an appointment with destiny." I don't think it got to David's head because he wasn't walking around like royalty afterwards. In fact, he was teased and pushed around by his brothers, and disrespected in the family. And not only that—you know the story of David and Goliath—after all that, he winds up being on the run from Saul. So just because he was anointed by that prophet, didn't mean that he was going to profit from it anytime soon.

But it seems the case that God does have His appointments for people. And, if you can imagine the better part of 13 years after, David was busy taking flight from Saul; actually, 13 years on the run and finally this man comes into his destiny—at least the first step of it, when elders gather together at Hebron and appoint David as king and anoint him.

This story is told in 2 Samuel chapter 5 verse 3, and it reads like this, "Therefore all the elders of Israel came to the king at Hebron, and King David made a covenant with them at Hebron before the Lord. And they anointed David king over Israel."

This actually came to him in stages. In fact, David's life came to him in stages. First, he's anointed by the prophet when he's a teenager, and then 13 years on the run from Saul who is mercilessly pursuing him. And now, in the wake of Saul's death—and David's going to grieve his death and not participate in it, though he could have on more than one occasion—finally, it begins to come to him. We're told first that here at Hebron, from where he's going to administrate for a number of years, the *Zekeenim* / the elders (the word "elder," *Zeke'een* in Hebrew, is "bearded one") and what happens is that those with *zekeh* / with smarts, realize—they come to terms with who this man is—and they acknowledge him. And David is anointed. And we see that he comes into his kingdom in stages.

I think this is a good point to underscore the fact that a lot of times people come into their victories in stages. This is important to underscore in a world where we microwave everything. We want it immediately: instant happiness, instant fortune, instant success in life. We want to believe God's promises for our life, but we want them instantly. The problem with that is that in reality, it's just not like that. You might find a church that will blow stardust in your face and tell you that success in life is yours just for sitting in the pew for a couple of weeks and putting your money in the offering plate. But I think that's overly simplistic, personally. To my way of thinking, if something sounds too good to be true, it probably is.

When we look at the story of David, we learn of a man who had many trials on the way to the top. And here I am, not at the top but close to the top, making my way up this little mount here that takes me up to where the Temple Mount is. This is the place—actually—where David later on is going to make his name known through his capital city here in Jerusalem.

As we look into David's world—and we've been doing that generally, but particularly in this program—we begin by looking at his anointing. And then we'll finish up by looking at David's excitement when the Ark was brought into his city. He was just so ecstatic. And why is that?

The Warrior King

Because David had a lot of challenges in his life, but he learned through it all, that if he would follow the Lord, the Lord would lead him on successfully. Like Paul said, "Thanks be to God who always leads us in triumph." And I'm reminded of that when I stand in the ancient City of David.

The Celebrated Warrior King

David's Conquest of Jerusalem

Almost directly beneath me, in the City of David, is a very famous tunnel, one that David remembered his entire life. And why is that? Because after he was anointed king at Hebron, it came to him to contend for the City of Jerusalem.

We're told in this chapter, that we began reading in the previous segment (2 Samuel 5), verse 6 and on, that David wanted Jerusalem. And the *Yebusi* / the Jebusites taunted him saying, This dog will never be able to enter into our stronghold. They had the high place. It was well fortified. But the Lord gave David a strategy, not just a vision... — He had a vision for a capital city, and after taking it, by the way, we're told that the Lord made his name great.

Actually it's the way this section finishes up in verse 10: "So David went on and became great," there from his capital city. — ...But the Lord didn't just give him a vision. He gave him a strategy for accomplishing it. Why is that? Because the road to success in life is marked with many perils. It seems that success doesn't just open up to us magically. I know you may well find a church or some place to sit, and the preacher will say, "Just believe this doctrine, and sit here, and put your money in the offering plate, and presto! Life is just going to come up good for you." Well, I do believe that God has a good plan for our life, to be sure. But coming here, from the City of David, coming here from just atop the tunnel that his men went into to fight, I want to tell you that while God has a good plan for us, it still is incumbent upon us to contend for it. If we want to be David-like leaders, it seems to me that—especially, by the way, in the day and time in which we live—I believe that godly people need to recover that contending. Why is that? Because we have work to do.

My concern is, frankly, that Christian faith and virtue are getting away from us. I believe that our government is getting away from us. I believe that family values are getting away from us. I believe that personal righteousness is getting away from us. And we need to have that militant edge, and be given to contending for our destiny in God. I believe those that are thus minded can enjoy good success by virtue of their being armed with that particular disposition.

In any case, here we're looking at a story where David tells his men, Let's arm up and go for it, guys. There's a vision and a strategy, he says in verse 7. Verse 6 ends with: They said, "David can't come here." But David, on the other hand, "took the stronghold of Zion," we're told. He took it. He seized it. David said on that day, "Whoever climbs up by way of the water shaft (just beneath me here) and defeats them, [he shall be chief and captain]" Well, this is where command is. Success in life, we're told in the Text, is going to go to those who contend for it.

Now, I want you to hear me on this, please. I believe that in America we have it way too easy, and many of us are way too spoiled. We think we're entitled to success in life. David didn't just give away commands in his army. They went to the brave. They went to the courageous. They went to those who wanted to serve him, and who, by bent of determination, armed up for the struggle and took some risks in order to accomplish it. And God was with them. And David honored that. Why is that? Because fundamentally he was that. And what's "that"? An entrepreneurial spirit, someone with a winning attitude, someone who wants to please God and go for it, to stand for something, to go against something, to contend, to press in. Where is "that"?

By the way, I believe that we need "that" now more than ever. The males in our culture are enculturated into being effeminate: worriers not warriors. We need to have that believing, that going for it, that dogged determination to believe God for a great future to serve, to carve out space in this world. I love the ilk who still believe. Even in a difficult Goliath-like world, I believe that David-like folk can have success in life. And I'm reminded of that as I sit in this historic place made famous because of the bravery and courage of David and his men many thousands of years ago.

The Warrior King

David Brings the Ark to Jerusalem

Tough guy though he most certainly was, he didn't do a very good job of containing himself, now did he? He invoked the ire of his wife who thought he was playing the fool in front of the masses. And why is that? It's because David was so very ecstatic when the Ark was brought into the city, he was beside himself. And the reason is because he knew that it was the Lord who placed him where he was. He credited the Lord with his success. The Lord gave him favor, with the net result that he was able to carve out a kingdom.

And here we are right now in the place where he made his name to dwell, here in the City of David. This is just one little corner of a big archaeological site. Friends, I'm coming to you from the palace of David, if you can imagine that. Oh, the place is abuzz with activity. Now, tourists can't come right here. We're beneath the scaffolding. We got permission to come and take you where people don't venture to go; but that's a Zola Levitt trademark, isn't it?

The Celebrated Warrior King

We have a cistern over here, various storerooms, restrooms, bedrooms, living rooms, closets, whatever—whatever the stuff a palace is made of, David's palace in particular. Here we are.

I'd like you to turn in your Bibles, please. We're told in 2 Samuel chapter 6 verse 14 that "David danced before the Lord with all his might." And then in verse 15, "David and all his house brought the Ark of the Lord with shouting and with the sound of a trumpet." And in verse 16 we're told that his wife sees him whirling around with abandon, and she despises him in her heart as a result.

Now, let me speak to you about this for a second. It seems to me that David wasn't just the kind of guy whose wife dragged him to church on Sundays. Well, it wasn't a church back then. …it's not like his wife was nudging him. Usually it's the lady of the house who's religious and the guy just gets shooed along for the sake of the kids or whatever. No, this is a guy who really is thrilled. David seems to be experiencing an ecstatic moment here: There's abandon, he doesn't really care what his wife thinks or what people think, he just so excited. Why is that? Because David, more than anyone, credits God with his success in life.

I want you to hear me on this, please. For some people it's just a religious tradition, but I believe that if we'll walk with God…. It's not an easy road and it's not a quick road, but you're going to be better off in life if you walk with Him than if you disregard Him and just break out your own machete and carve a path in the wilderness of this world. David learned that.

The Warrior King

We began this program by reminding you that though David had his challenges—first with his family who didn't believe in him, and then Goliath and his brothers taunt him out there on the field, and then he runs from Saul, if you can imagine that, 13 years on the run! But you know what?— God used the experience to build him up.

Now, I want you to hear me. I believe that we have a God who leads us in triumph. I believe that the males of our species need to recover that kind of triumphalism, that believing God for great things. I want you to know that if we put God first…. There's a verse that Yeshua said, that if we seek first God's kingdom and His righteousness, then other things would be added unto us (Matthew 6:33).

Here in the City of David that was carved out many years ago, I'm reminded of the fact that this God who's the same today, yesterday, and forever, wants to make a name for anyone who wants to cast their name among His disciples. And why don't you do that? I believe that we live in Goliath-like times, that David-like men and women who stand up and contend—I believe, that we—can expect good things from God even in a world where good news is in high demand but short supply.

Speaking of "good things to come," how David points to the best coming news of all is noted in the following chapter.

6

David: A Messianic Prototype

David in Isaiah

I recently filmed at one of the most fantastic finds in biblical archaeology. In the '40s a Bedouin discovered scrolls that hit the world by storm. And you're looking at a facsimile here. Actually, I am in the Shrine of the Book. And here we're looking at an ancient book, the book of Isaiah, copied by the sectaries of Qumran many years ago.

Isaiah was a fascinating personality, and he's worth considering when we consider *David Melech* / King David. Though Isaiah himself wasn't part of David's administration, actually, he wished he was. And the reason was because Isaiah made his entrance onto the stage of the human drama during the administration of *Yoshiyahu*, a king who started off good enough, but a king who went bad. He went south. Isaiah saw his demise, and it's recorded in the book of Kings and the book of Chronicles. Not only is it recorded, but it said as much that Isaiah was the historian who talked about the demise of Judah under Josiah's ministration. And it's perhaps for that reason that when Isaiah began his *prophetic* administration, he spoke to the *pathetic* first. You can't read the first five chapters of Isaiah without your toes curling in your shoes when you hear his harsh invective, his diatribe, how that prophet gave voice to a world gone bad. Priests, the religious, the secular, everyone who was anyone was on the take.

Against the backdrop of that Draconian introduction, in the 11th chapter, as we see here, Isaiah spoke of a coming king, a David-like king. We're told in chapter 11, "there will come forth a rod from the stump of Jesse, and a branch will grow from his roots." Remember that Jesse is David's father. And the Davidic House, in effect, was cut down. But there would emerge from it a righteous branch, a Righteous One, a *Mashiach* / a Messianic character. We're told here that the *Ruach Ha-Adonai* / "the Spirit of the Lord will rest upon Him, The Spirit of wisdom and understanding," counsel, might, knowledge, fear of the Lord. "His delight will be in the fear of the Lord." *Vaya'ar Adonai* / the fear of the Lord doesn't speak of trepidation and panic as much as it does of respect. And because He respects the Lord, He respects others.

Isaiah was chagrined. And why is that? Because the kingdom was vitiated; it was defiled beneath the hands of godless rulers. He says in 10:2, they "robbed the needy of justice. They take what is right from the poor of my people. The widows are their prey." He goes on in the 10th chapter

David: A Messianic Prototype

verses 2 and 12 to say that people are robbed of their treasuries, again like our world where the wicked take advantage of the weaker. Isaiah sees a David-like leader who re-emerges even centuries after David, and this is the Messianic personality. We're told here that His delight will be in the fear of the Lord, and He will rule with justice and equity and fairness and goodness. Now, listen to me. We need that kind of godly leadership in our godless world. And I am concerned, personally. I don't know what you look for in leadership, be it civil or religious, but personally, individuals who resonate with Judeo-Christian ethics really matter to me. And when I don't see that, I am gravely concerned.

Isaiah pointed to the day when…—You know, even David's bones were already parched and dry for centuries—…but he points to the day when Someone would emerge likened unto David. And this reflects the fact that, among other things, the memory of David is alive. And may the memory be alive in our day, as we are, with some measure of anxiety, looking into the future. May it be your prayer with mine that godly people will wield influence in our culture to the end that we may be better by virtue of their so doing.

The Warrior King

David in Jeremiah

Not far from where the Dead Sea Scrolls are housed is a scale version of the City of David, in *Yerushalayim* / in Jerusalem. Folks spent a small fortune to reconstruct that. And it's beautiful. I am told by a friend, Elia Sides, that this site is, along with Masada, one of the most frequented sites that pilgrims want to check into when they visit Israel, and they're excited to see it.

Yirmyah / Jeremiah, however, looked at this portion of the city and he was not a happy camper. And why is that? Well, *Yirmyah* / Jeremiah is on record saying, in the 23rd chapter of his own book, "Woe to the shepherds who destroy and scatter the sheep." *Yirmyah* / Jeremiah saw destruction coming upon the City of David. *Yerushalayim* was going to take a hit by the Babylonians. And why is that? Because Jeremiah says the priests were vitiated and defiled. The secular rulers were defiled as well. In so many ways, it was a world like our own. That is to say, there was the pretense of religion and virtue, but the world had long

David: A Messianic Prototype

since abandoned biblical ethics. And so it is that *Yirmyah* / Jeremiah was on record as saying the sheep are going to be scattered, and so they were.

That's the bad news. The good news, however, is that Jeremiah envisioned a good world to come. And I'm glad he did, by the way. He didn't just leave his constituents despairing, as we're going to see in a moment when we look in the Bible, though he himself despaired. Jeremiah is called "the weeping prophet." He's so very infusive, emotive. He's weeping. Why? Because he sees this beauty falling apart. He's called "the lonely prophet," as well. And why is that? Because this priestly prophet was told never to marry and bear children. Why is that? Because the children were destined for the slave market—if not death outright—when the Babylonians were going to come and rape and pillage and plunder, and come they did.

Yirmyah / Jeremiah, as I said, saw a bad moon rising over this world that, sadly, is so much like our own. Happily however, he telescopes to the future. And he sees a bright spot beginning to emerge over the horizon, like the sun rising from the east, displacing the prevailing darkness. He says in verse 5, in his own words, "'Behold, the days are coming', says the Lord, 'when I will raise up to David a Branch of righteousness.'" We heard in the Isaianic passage earlier about the *netzer* / the branch that will spring forth. And, by the way, that's why in the New Testament, Jesus is associated with the city called *Natzeret* / Nazareth. It's named after the same. That connection wouldn't have been lost to Jewish people in the first century of this, the Common Era.

61

The Warrior King

In any case, Jeremiah telescopes into the future, and he sees this Davidic person coming. David's been dead for years by the time he speaks. And David's been dead now for millennia; but even in the Jewish world today, we sing *David Melech Yisrael chai* / "David, the king of Israel lives." And why is that? Because the memory lives. And why is that? Because the prophets kept his memory alive. And why is that? Because, against the backdrop of a decaying world, they saw there would be an emergent, David-like leader. We're told in verse 6, "In His days, Judah will be saved." And he says, under His administration "Israel will dwell securely." And then he goes on to speak of this leader, and says, "And this is the name by which He shall be called: *Adonai Tsidkenu,* the Lord Our Righteousness."

I don't know how you feel, but in many ways I'm discouraged. When I look out—I'm not the wisest owl in the forest—but when I look out over my perch, I'm not a happy camper when I look at our own culture. I see an abandonment of Judeo-Christian ethics. I see a pretense of religion, but people denying the power of it. I find people talking the talk, but I find rot and decay. And frankly, I find it in high places. Like Jeremiah, and like you perhaps, I, we, he look forward to the day when we'll see this emergent leadership. This series is called *The Warrior King,* and we're looking for David-like leadership in Goliath-like times. May it be that, more and more, women and men stand up for biblical virtue in a world where that virtue is in very high demand and very short supply.

If, like me, you long for the day when the "Prince of Peace" will make peace, please accept my invitation to contend for the Prince's arrival in advance of His coming.

David in Ezekiel

I filmed a program from the Kidron Valley. To my left, the ancient Temple once stood—and now there are Turkish walls 'round about it; to my right, the Mount of Olives. There I was in a valley where shepherds used to frequent, verdant lands; but that was yesteryear. Behind me that day was a monument to an unpleasant name, one that's not often repeated in Israel. It's a monument to Absalom; and why he would be remembered in a place like this is anybody's guess. Why is that? Because, truth be known, he himself is *persona non grata*. And why is that? Because Absalom was David's son who sought to kill him. He drove David out of his own palace, made the king run for his life in the later years of his life. As Absalom—the name *Avi* means "my father," and *shalom* is "peace." He has a name connected to peace, "My father is peace"—But he gave his father *surus*, truth be known. *Surus*—he gave him "aggravation" as he sought to undermine him.

The Warrior King

David lived in a precarious world. This Absalom scattered the sheep, drove David away, and caused angst in the culture. And you know what? When there's bad leadership that comes to power, it does much the same. David must have been spellbound with grief when he considered what had happened: not only his own political dislocation, but the fact that his own son, his wicked son—who killed his brother previously, by the way—that he has come to power. And David was not a happy camper.

Ezekiel remembers this story years later, that is to say, the David story. Ezekiel inhabited a world much like David did in the sense that bad people had come to power. In fact, the wound in Judah was irreparable. It was not to be fixed. Judgment was meted out. And why is that? Because wickedness reigned from the palace, wickedness reigned from the pulpit, and wickedness was ubiquitous in the pew everywhere. And it was not to be fixed. So much for the bad news.

In a world where the righteous were disconcerted and scattered, Ezekiel telegraphed out into the future, and he envisioned that a Good Shepherd will emerge. He lambasts, in the 34th chapter, "It's these bad shepherds that are heaving discontent in the culture!" But then he goes on to say, in verse 23, and I quote, he says, "I will establish one shepherd over them, and he shall feed them—My servant David." David was long since dead as of Ezekiel's writing. But the memory of this imperfect and righteous sort…. He knew what it was to repent. He found repentance. He was a man after God's own heart. Ezekiel says, "We need some of that ruling again."

David: A Messianic Prototype

Now, arguably, Ezekiel is looking forward. His forward thrust to this coming Davidic Shepherd harks to the Messianic era. We know that, by the way, because when we look in the New Testament in the Mattean gospel—the Matthew Text—that was written in the Semitic language, originally it opens up,

זה ספר תולדת המשיח ישוע בן־דוד בן־אברהם

Zeh sefer toldot Ha-Mashiach Yeshua ben David ben Avraham.

He's introduced,

ben David ben Avraham
"the son of David."

And we know in the New Testament that as Yeshua went about, "Son of David! Son of David!" Well, here Ezekiel envisions that a Davidic Son will emerge, and we're told, "He will be their Shepherd." And then in verse 24, "And I, the Lord, will be their God, and My servant David a prince among them; I, the Lord, have spoken."

I don't know about you, but that's what I want. I look forward to the day when *Sar Shalom* / the Prince of Peace comes. But until such time as He arrives, I want David-like leadership in Goliath-like times ruling in our land. I want that man after God's own heart. I believe politicians, frankly, can be very well intended. But I believe, as well, that the road to hell is paved with good intentions. I want praying people ruling. You and I need to pray for our country, for our culture, because we want godly leadership—and we need it—because we need David-like leadership in these Goliath-like times. When the righteous are in power, it's sweet music to my ears.

The Warrior King

7

Israel's Sweet Psalmist

David and the Psalms I

Bible readers are informed that music has been around since the dawn of Creation. In the Hebrew book *Bereshit /* Genesis, in the 4th chapter in the 23rd verse, readers are informed that one of Cain's progeny, a fellow named Jubal, was the father of those who played the harp. Not only were people into music at the beginning, but even before the beginning of time (according to the Hebrew Bible) music was around. Why do I say that? Well, I don't say that. Ezekiel was speaking of Satan. This inherently evil personality goes by the Latin epithet *Lucifer*, or light bearer, who deceives. And we're told in chapter 28 verse 13 that he, this personality, was in Eden, the Garden of God. *Paradise* is the Latin word for "enclosed garden,"

and there he was, and from there he fell. The reason why I mention that in conjunction with music is to say that this same person, we're told, came into his own. In Ezekiel chapter 28 verse 13, he says, "The workmanship of timbrels and pipes was prepared for him on the day that he was created." Hence, you have some correlation between this evil personality and the manufacture and the development of music. But, as the old saying goes, why should the devil have all the good music? Enter David.

Actually, we see music before David. Miriam—after *Moshe Rabbeinu* / after Moses—and Israel, they make their way through the sea. The waters part. We're told in the book *Shemot* / in Exodus that she comes out with tambourine. We find primitive starbursts of praise accompanied with musical instrumentation.

We then, as we make our way through the Hebrew Bible, find that primitive music evolves and becomes more formalized by the time we get to the book *Tehillim* / Psalms. The word *psalms* comes from the word *psalter*. They're cut from the same cloth. It's a prayer book. The Hebrew *tehillim* means "praises." Actually, it's not one book. It's five. Inasmuch as you have the five books of Moses, you have five books of worship in the Hebrew Bible. And some of these worship songs come with what today are anachronistic, hard-to-come-to-terms-with archaic expressions, various forms of musical notations that reflected that in antiquity we had Levitical choirs. In the Old Testament economy, they were given to giving voice to biblical praise. And why is that? Because it was long observed that music enabled individuals to rise above their vexing circumstances. Music provides a mechanism to put prayer to song with instrumentation. It helps people to pray.

Israel's Sweet Psalmist

It helps people give expression to things they're thinking and they're feeling.

It seems that the Lord led David into that world early, and I'm glad that the Lord did. We're all the beneficiaries of the Warrior King's musical proclivity. David loved the Lord and he loved to give voice. There are some 70 psalms that attest to that.

I remember years ago, I was paralyzed from the neck down. I had picked up a dread disease called Guillain-Barré. I couldn't walk. I could barely move a hand, a finger. And someone brought me a CD player. And there was a song in there by Paul Wilbur, "I Will Lift Up My Eyes Unto The Lord." And with my finger I'd play it and push replay, and play it and replay. And why is that? Because, at that time, this is the only thing I could lift. And I'd cry, and I'd pray, and I'd sing. Once, I was in a lawsuit as well, pressed against the wall in a world gone bad, dealing with wicked situations. I'd have to pray the psalms every morning, to tell you the truth, just to get my head above the water.

Well, thank God for God; thank God for David; thank God for that gift. Different people have been the beneficiary of it. Saul himself, we're told in the Text in 1 Samuel chapter 16, he'd get wrapped around the axle. He was very disconcerted and depressed. And David would come and play his music and, you know, it tamed the savage beast. I have seen untamed beasts, however, and can tell you that the sights they leave in their wake are not pleasant to behold.

The Warrior King

David and the Psalms II

I've seen this on more than one occasion. And what am I
talking about? The aftermath of violence. What am I
referencing? A crime scene. As a police officer in another
career, I've walked into worlds where they use knives,
pistols, shotguns, and they've killed. It's horrible, at one
level, what happens. When I think of the pent-up energies.
People can't control them. The rage gets the better of them,
and they unleash it on those 'round about them. And it's
not pretty. What they leave in their aftermath is pillage.
And so it is, we walk into a world here now, and now I am
speaking as a biblical theologian, not as a police officer.
We walk into a world here where we experience David,
who's the victim of someone's malice. What do I mean by
that? Saul is hellbent on destroying him. He takes a spear
and thrusts it at him. And you know, I wonder, David must
have thought, "Why?"

But it wasn't the first time, mind you. Recall the story
when David began his fighting career, if you will. He goes

to the battle lines to bring food staples to his brothers. Goliath shows up, and David's "What's up with this? Someone ought to tell him to shut up." And his brothers say, "Why don't you shut up, David, and go back to your stupid little sheep?" And David says something that he must have thought on many occasions: "What did I do?" The reason why I say that is, surely David—the heroic David—when the world collapses 'round about him, David must have surely thought, "What did I do? What did I do to deserve this?" Like Jesus, on more than one occasion, he must have, at the feeling level, said, "My God, my God, why hast Thou forsaken me?" Because it sure felt like that. And why is that? Because trusted people 'round about had forsaken Him, to put it mildly.

David had to run for his own sake, if you will. And this is interesting for my money. David, this guy who's going to go on from Saul, when he's going to look at his career as he's reflecting on it at the very end of it, he's going to prove to be Israel's greatest Warrior King. This is a guy who inhabits real estate that has 6,000 square miles, and when he's done, Israel has expanded to 60,000 square miles. This is a winner, not a loser. But it's interesting that David spent the beginning of his career on the run. This forward-moving king spent 13 years—talk about 13 being an unlucky number!—13 years on the run from Saul for no good reason.

Now, I want you to hear me on this. This isn't a nice thing to say, at one level. It's typically what's *not* said from pulpits or on Christian TV. But I don't construe myself as typical. And I want you to hear me on this. There may be some of you who have a "Saul" in your world, that is to say, within your webs of relationships, someone who's not just frustrating, but someone who's detrimental to your health, who's threatening you. And listen! When I'm reading the biblical story, I'm reminded that sometimes you have to put it in reverse. David, who was minded to begin his career by serving Saul, realized that he had to get out of Dodge. There may be some within the sound of my voice who might construe that as wisdom for you. I know there's a song in the church, "Something tells me I'm in for something good." But when it comes to this domestic violence stuff, when it repeats, and goes over and over again, something tells me that you're *not*. I want to tell you, with the Bible in one hand and a little Jesus in my heart, that sometimes it's time to say, "Goodbye." But for fear of an uncertain future, I've seen people hold on to the very end, leading to their own death, because they didn't know when to cut and get out of Dodge.

I want you to hear me, please. Uncertain as David's world was when bad things were happening around him, I want you to know that he walked by faith into an uncertain future. And you know what happened? God raised him up to be something that was greater than his wildest imagination, at the time when he was dodging those spears. I want you to know that the same God is the God of David. The same God is the God for you. And I want you to know that the same Lord is the Lord of all, and He bestows His riches upon all who call upon Him. I believe that God has a great future for you, and He can use even the difficulties in the present to prepare you for it.

David and the Psalms III

David cut his teeth working as a shepherd. I think it's for that reason that David was able to make the shift and envision that "the Lord is *my* shepherd." Inasmuch as he himself was kindly disposed toward the welfare of those under his charge, he knew that God would do similar on his behalf. It's for that reason, in part, where in Psalm 34—and I really want you to turn there with me and have a look, if you will, please. He says in Psalm 34 in verse 4, "I sought the Lord, and He heard me, and He delivered me from my fears."

In the previous segment we considered that David was pressed against the turbulence of trying times. But he had a good God who was a good shepherd, and he says, "I sought Him and He delivered me." It goes on to say, "They looked to Him and were radiant, and their faces were not ashamed." Our Warrior King learned that he could look to God, even crying out from his difficulties, and God could take away the shame and the difficulty and give him a kind of joy.

73

The Warrior King

There is a peace of God that passes all understanding, and our Warrior King learned about that.

He says, "This poor man cried out, and the Lord heard him, and He saved him from all of his troubles." Whether it's Saul, whether it's Goliath, whether it's his own sins, our hero learned that there's a good God who loves him, who was willing and able to save him from all of his troubles, much as a shepherd who's kindly disposed toward sheep will lead them on successfully. And when the enemies come 'round about—snakes, wolves, whatever—that shepherd's going to take care of them as well.

This poor man cried to the Lord and He delivered him. Then he says a statement in verse 7 that's as true for him as it is for me, as it is for you: "The angel of the Lord encamps around those who fear Him, and delivers them." I believe, by the way, that we don't just have some philosophical society. I believe that we have a God who is willing and able. In John chapter 10, Jesus said, "I am the door. Anyone who enters by me will be saved, and will go in and out and find pasture." And the word "saved" in the Greek means to deliver, to heal, to make whole. We have a God who really cares about us. We have a verse in Scripture, "Thanks be to God who always leads us in triumph," said Paul, who had it in a bad way on more than one day. But, God is good. We're told here as well…well, we're encouraged here in verse 8, "Oh taste and see that the Lord is good. Blessed is the man [or the woman] who trusts in Him."

Our Warrior King learned that he could come up from nowhere. He came from obscurity as a young man tending his father's sheep, a dad that didn't respect him much. And then he entered into a world where a surrogate dad, if you will, Saul, took him under his charge. And it wasn't just disrespect. It was out and outright hate. David cut his teeth in his trials. He learned that there's a good God who watches over his Word to perform it. And David's story, as he makes his way from the womb to tomb, is telling because in so many ways he's like us. And he has commended his recipe for success in life.

You know, there can be families today that come from the old country, and there are grandma's recipes. And goodness, if we could just learn to cook like that, we would eat well! In much the same way, David's recipes for success in life were left in his own words. He talks about fearing the Lord, seeking Him. Difficulties notwithstanding, we learn about a God who leads us in triumph. It says here, "Oh fear the Lord." Now, that means revere Him, respect Him. "Oh fear the Lord, you his saints." That's more than just going to church on Sundays and on weekends and if there's something that interests you. A reverence for the Lord pays dividends. Our Warrior King learned that. We're considering David-like leadership in Goliath-like times, and we're learning about a God who loves, who saves, who redeems. He did it for David. He'll do it for you.

The Warrior King

8

David: Prototype of Israel's Messiah

David in Jesus' Line

Raised in a Jewish family, I can't tell you how surprised I was—finally one day I opened up the "Christian" Bible and discovered that it's a very Jewish story. The New Testament in Hebrew is the *Brit Hadasha* / the new covenant. While it's "new" at one level, it's not brand new. The reason why I say that is, if you look at the New Testament, you have a lot of carry over there from themes that resonated in the Old Testament Text. The Hebrew Bible closes with unappeased longings, unfulfilled prophecies, expectations yet to have been realized. The Old Testament comes to a close with a prophecy unfulfilled given to David. In 2 Samuel chapter 7, the promise was that a special leader was going to come from Davidic linage. Not long after that, we see a long crumble

and tumble as Israelite culture falls apart. It's racked by
political intrigue, unrest. Sin, like a boa constrictor, wraps
itself around the commonwealth and squeezes the life out
of it.

The New Testament opens up in the Mattean Gospel—the
Gospel of Matthew—in Hebrew,

זה ספר תולדת המשיח ישוע בן־דוד בן־אברהם

Zeh sefer toldot Ha-Mashiach Yeshua ben David ben Avraham
"the book of the genealogy of Jesus the Messiah, the Son
of David, the Son of Abraham."

I'm coming to you from Israel right now, and in this
country today there are people who would make me feel
guilty if they had their way. "Oh, you're a Jew. You can't
believe in Jesus." And I could go to Rome, I imagine, or
other places, and there would be Christian people who
would say, "Oh, you can't be Jewish." And the reason is
because there's a chasm that's alleged. There's the Jewish
world over here, and the Jesus world over there, and they
just don't belong together.

Well, hear me please. If that's true, then Matthew never got
the memo, because when I read my Bible, the first breath of
the story connects Jesus to the Jews through the Old
Testament's most famous Jew, or at least one of them,
David. There are so many chapters written about him and
by him. He's right up there at the top of the list. I grew up
singing his praises. *David Melech Yisrael chai vikayam* /
"David the king of Israel lives forever." And there are
songs today in Hebrew, *Melech ozair u'Moshiach, u'Magen*
/ "King, redeemer, savior, and shield." All this harks back
to David, who captured the imagination of a people, loved
God, sought God—a kingdom builder who carved out

space on planet Earth where God's will and ways resonate. David!

And we look in the New Testament and learn that his offspring, his most famous offspring, makes His entrance onto the stage of the human drama. But, like David himself, He came into a troubled world. Why do I say that? Well, *Yosef*, His step-dad, was rather troubled. And why is that? We read in Matthew chapter one that he learns that his girlfriend, his fiancée, Miriam, has come up pregnant—and he knew he wasn't the guy! He's minded to divorce her, but wanting to do it quietly.

What happens is that he's visited by an angel. The word "angel" in Hebrew, *malach*, comes from a eucharitic verb which means "to send." God dispatches a messenger to *Yosef*. What does he tell him? In verse 20, he says, "The angel of the Lord appeared to him in a dream saying, "*Yosef ben David* / Joseph, son of David, do not be afraid to take Miriam as your wife." He did just that, and the rest is history.

We've been looking at David in this series, but now, as we wrap up on David, we want to look at David's most famous son. We want to consider *Yeshua* / Jesus, of Davidic extract, who personifies all that was good about David, and more. Inasmuch as David brought about deliverance in the Old Testament, so too we learn about One presaged in the synagogue's literature who would enlighten humans and bring about peace on Earth and good will toward men.

The Warrior King

Gabriel Informs Mary She will Bring Forth a Son Named Jesus

In Luke chapter 2 verse 32, Jesus is described as "a light to bring revelation to the gentiles," and He's noted as being "the glory of Your people Israel." Personally, I believe we live in a world where people have come to terms with the fact that He's the "light to bring revelation to the gentiles," although I'm not altogether sure people know what that means. But I do believe we live in a world where fallen off the cliff is the notion that this Jesus is the glory of the People of Israel.

As for the first point, Him being a light to bring revelation to the gentiles, I'm not altogether sure that everyone has come to terms with the fact that Jesus can give revelation to individuals. People need to be born anew, receive him in their hearts, and then there's an inner light, if you will. And people, when they face vexing circumstances, can hear a voice within them saying, "This is the way. Walk in it." As people cultivate the Christian life, they can then have

David: Prototype of Israel's Messiah

revelation to give them answers for the vexing troubles of the day. Some people have a superficial kind of worship of Jesus without coming to terms with the nature of what it is to be "born again" and have the Spirit within, and thus to have revelation to "lead us on into triumph."

Issues with that aside, I do know that fallen off the cliff, as I'd said, is the sense that Jesus is, in fact, the glory of the People of Israel. And this is tragic, I believe. In Luke chapter 1 verse 26, Luke considers Jesus' origin. There's a story here of an angel, Gabriel, who visits a Jewess named Miriam. "Miriam" comes from the Hebrew word *mar* which means "bitterness" or "sorrow," and *yam* which means "sea"—sea of sorrows. It might be an appropriate name. She was carrying the world on her shoulders when she learned that she, oops!...came up pregnant through the agency of the *Ruach Ha-Kodesh* [the Holy Spirit]. Completely unexpected. Here's a young girl, and this has all happened upon her. She is perplexed and she carries it in her heart, trying to sort out what it all means. We're told here that her husband was trying to sort it out as well. As we saw in the previous segment, he gets a visitation.

Here, the messenger visits Miriam personally, and tells her what she may well sense. In verse 31, "You will conceive in your womb and bring forth a Son." And then we're told in 32 and 33 that "He will be great and will be called the Son of the Highest; and the Lord will give Him the throne of His father David" —see, Yeshua is an extension of David— and that "He will reign over the house of Jacob forever, and of His kingdom there will be no end." If I read the Bible correctly, Miriam is informed that the *Mashiach* / the Messiah for the world is going to come through her.

81

The Warrior King

Inasmuch as David was promised in 2 Samuel chapter 7—
you can look it up, verses 12 and 13—that the special Son
was going to come and be assigned a throne and a household
and a dominion to reign forever, here you look into the New
Testament story—in the Christian Bible, or what's construed
as the non-Jewish Bible—to hear about the coming of the
Savior of the world. The way the story unfolds in its own
context, is that yes, this is the Savior of the world, but this
person is the glory of the Jewish world. Today in Israel, if a
rabbi came forth and had one one-thousandth the influence
that Jesus had....

If you look at the Jesus story, the genius here is that we're
taking the Jewish Bible, and we're getting into the hearts
and minds of billions on planet Earth. And this is facilitated
through a Jesus experience. Jesus is the principal interpreter
as individuals look at the New Testament and get some
sense of how to interpret the Old Testament by virtue of
their so doing. If there was any Jewish rabbi in the world
today who exacted this kind of influence, he would be
heralded as the best thing since the invention of wheat
bread, the best Jewish scholar since Moses. Jesus was the
greatest Jew who ever lived. He came with a prophecy
attached to Him, and that is that He would bring revelation
to the gentiles and be the glory of the People of Israel.

I believe today, that we need David-like leadership for
Goliath-like times. Individuals need the Son of David in
their hearts because He can bring revelation. That is to say,
if you're vexed with challenges, He can give you insights
and give you a Word so you'll know how to walk through
it, onward to a glorious and successful future—and what a
future it is!

Wise Men Visit Mary and the Infant Jesus

When we worship Him, we "prime the pump" to facilitate the outpouring of His grace. The word "worship" comes from an expression "a ship of worth." It means to ascribe value to something. You might be familiar with the story when these individuals come, these men from the East. What do they do? They give gold, frankincense, and myrrh, and they lay them down at the feet of a young king named *Yeshua* / Jesus. The reason why I mention that at this juncture is because we live in a world today when individuals similarly come and give gifts, and they lay them down at the feet of this Davidic king, whom we refer to as Jesus, or, in the Hebrew, *Yeshua*, the son of David / *ben David*.

He's introduced in the New Testament as the Son of David, and we've introduced you to David, or reintroduced you or reacquainted you with David in the Hebrew Bible. What have we learned? We learned of a story of a young fellow who came out of obscurity—little known, disrespected. His own father didn't believe in him, and his brothers disrespected him. But, difficulties aside, he jumped into the fray. He cared about God. He cared about taking up Israel's burdens. He hated injustice. He went after it with verve and vitality. And, at the end of the day, the Lord used him to carve out a kingdom.

In this series, we've been concerned with David. We refer to him as the Warrior King. And over and again you've heard me talk about the need for David-like leadership in these Goliath-like times. That means different things in different contexts. For sure, I believe we do well if in government we're led by individuals with Judeo-Christian ethics. I love those values and virtues. Would that individuals were men and women after God's own heart. I believe that's a recipe for success, because the extent to which individuals are yielded to God's kingdom affords an opportunity for those biblical virtues to inform decision makers. I just think the world's a better place when decision makers have a place in their hearts for biblical values.

David-like leadership in Goliath-like times can refer to the smaller culture within the culture. There's the broader world culture, and then there's individual family culture. I believe that families need David-like leadership in Goliath-like times. Would that families learned to live by biblical virtue and vision. Would that families learned about forgiveness. Would that families learned the lessons that we find in the life of David. We could be spared many pains. I believe that families are the better when we take into account what we can learn from David's principles as well as what we can learn from his examples, both good and bad.

David: Prototype of Israel's Messiah

And then there are individuals. I believe that individuals need David-like leadership for Goliath-like times. And the way that happens is by individuals inviting the Son of David into their worlds. I believe that when we ask Jesus into our hearts, we're asking the Son of David to come into our hearts. And when we bow the knee to Him, we're bowing the knee to the reign of the Son of David. I believe that we need that. I believe that we need Him. I believe that we need God, and I believe that there's an offer on the table.

In this volume you've heard me talk about David, and as I bring it to a close, I want to talk to you about you. I want you to know that there's an offer on the table. The Hebrew Bible is opened up for all to see and experience now because of a Jew named Jesus whom I construe as the greatest Jewish man who ever lived. And He was more than a man. What He's done through the agency of His life and death and ministry and His resurrection, is afforded the opportunity for all people to open up the Bible and learn about the God of Israel, that God loves you. He has a wonderful plan for your life. If individuals would receive Him, if individuals would but embrace the principles found in His Book, then they would be strong. Over and again we find in the biblical Text how God raises up individuals, whether it's David, whether it's Abraham, whether it's you. It's not just about those guys. It's about you. The same Lord is Lord of all, and He bestows His riches upon all who call upon Him.

The Warrior King

David—A man after God's own heart!

David: Prototype of Israel's Messiah

The Warrior King

David: Prototype of Israel's Messiah

The Warrior King